Investigations

Changing Shape

Patricia Whitehouse

Raintree

www.raintreepublishers.co.uk
Visit our website to find out more information about **Raintree** books.

To order:
☎ Phone 44 (0) 1865 888112
📄 Send a fax to 44 (0) 1865 314091
💻 Visit the Raintree Bookshop at **www.raintreepublishers.co.uk** to browse our catalogue and order online.

First published in Great Britain by Raintree, Halley Court, Jordan Hill, Oxford OX2 8EJ, part of Harcourt Education.
Raintree is a registered trademark of Harcourt Education Ltd.

Editorial: Diyan Leake and Richard Woodham
Design: Michelle Lisseter
Picture Research: Maria Joannou
Production: Jonathan Smith

Originated by Dot Gradations Ltd
Printed and bound in Hong Kong, China by South China Printing Company

ISBN 1 844 43670 5
08 07 06 05 04
10 9 8 7 6 5 4 3 2 1

British Library Cataloguing in Publication Data
Whitehouse, Patricia
Changing Shape. – (Investigations)
620.1'12
A full catalogue record for this book is available from the British Library.

Acknowledgements
The publishers would like to thank the following for permission to reproduce photographs: Heinemann Library pp. **4–22** (Warling Studios).

Cover photograph of two people blowing up balloons reproduced with permission of Corbis (Tom and Dee Ann McCarthy).

Every effort has been made to contact copyright holders of any material reproduced in this book. Any omissions will be rectified in subsequent printings if notice is given to the publishers.

The paper used to print this book comes from sustainable resources.

❗ CAUTION: Children should be supervised by an adult when handling food and kitchen utensils.

Contents

Some words are shown in bold, **like this.**
You can find them in the glossary on page 23.

How can things change shape?

Lots of things can change shape.

You can use your hands to change the shape of some things.

There are other ways to make things change shape.

You can use air.

Can clay change shape?

Here is some clay.

It is the same shape as the can.

Press down on the clay with your hands.

Does it change shape?

Can the clay change back?

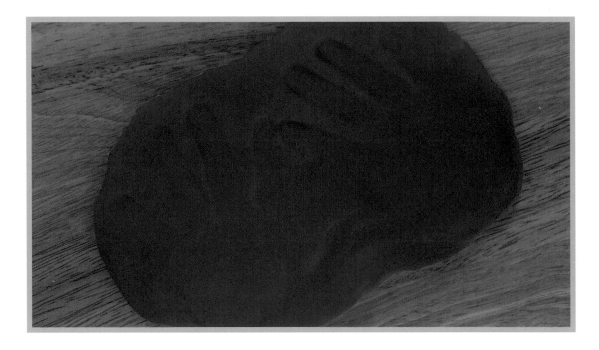

Now the clay is flat.

It has two hand shapes in it.

Push the clay back into the can.

It is the same shape as the
can again.

Can folding change paper?

This paper has a **triangle** shape.

It has three corners and three sides.

Fold the paper along the lines.

What happens to the shape?

Can the paper change back?

Now the paper has a **square** shape.

It has four corners and four sides.

Unfold the paper.

It has a **triangle** shape again.

Can cutting change paper?

This paper has a **rectangle** shape.

Use scissors to cut it along the line.

Now there are two pieces of paper.

They are both **triangle** shapes.

Can the paper change back?

Paper cannot change back after you cut it.

You can use sticky tape to **connect** the pieces together again.

Can stretching change a balloon?

This balloon is flat.

Blow it up.

Air stretches the balloon.

Now it is round.

Can the balloon change back?

Let the air out of the balloon.

What happens to its shape?

The balloon is flat again.

The air has stretched it out, though.

Quiz

What will this balloon look like when you blow it up?

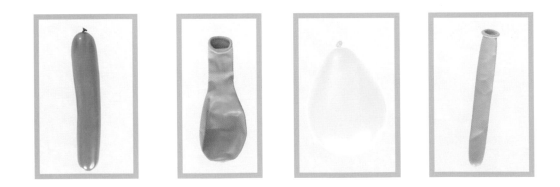

Look for the answer on page 24.

Glossary

connect
put two things together

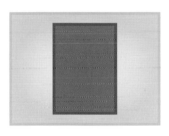

rectangle
shape with four corners and four sides

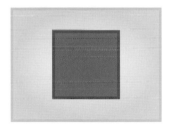

square
shape with four corners and four sides of the same length

triangle
shape with three corners and three sides

Index

Answer to quiz on page 22

The balloon will be big and yellow.

Titles in the Investigations series include:

Hardback   1 844 43670 5

Hardback   1 844 43671 3

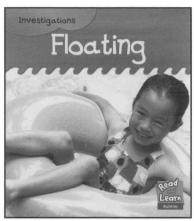

Hardback   1 844 21550 4

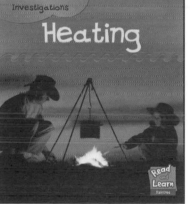

Hardback   1 844 43672 1

Hardback   1 844 43673 X

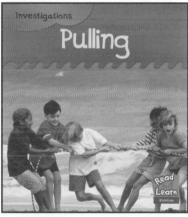

Hardback   1 844 21551 2

Hardback   1 844 21552 0

Hardback   1 844 21553 9

Hardback   1 844 21554 7

Find out about the other titles in this series on our website www.raintreepublishers.co.uk